THE ALL NEW STYLE OF MAGAZINE-BOOKS

ANNA MARIE
MAGAZINE

www.AnnaMarieGospel.com

MP

MOCY PUBLISHING
WWW.MOCYPUBLISHING.COM

Printed by CreateSpace, An Amazon.com Company

ANNA MARIE
MAGAZINE

EDITOR-IN-CHIEF
Anna Marie McCutchen
annamariepraise@gmail.com

EDITORAL DIRECTOR
Sheree Cranford
sheree@sdmlive.com

GRAPHIC/WEB DESIGNER
D. "Casino" Bailey
casino@sdmlive.com

A&R MANAGER
Anna Marie McCutchen
annamariepraise@gmail.com

ACCOUNT EXECUTIVE
Hil-Roe Productions

PHOTOGRAPHERS
KaSiris Martez Xavier
Casino Bailey

CONTRIBUTORS
Cleve People
Jimavis Arnold

COPY ORDERS & ADVERTISING OFFICE
Send Money Order or Check to:
Mocy Publishing
P.O. Box 35195
Detroit, Michigan 48235
(586) 646-8505
advertise@sdmlive.com

Copy Order Item #:
Anna Marie Magazine Issue #1 2016
S&H Plus Retail Price - $9.99 per copy

WWW.ANNAMARIEGOSPEL.COM

Printed by CreateSpace, An Amazon.com Company

MP
MOCY PUBLISHING

Copyright © 2016 Agent for Christ, LLC and
Mocy Publishing, LLC. All rights reserved.
Printed in the U.S.A.

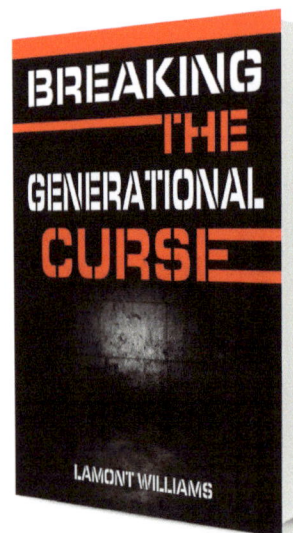

CONTENTS

WANNA BE HAPPY?
KIRK FRANKLIN

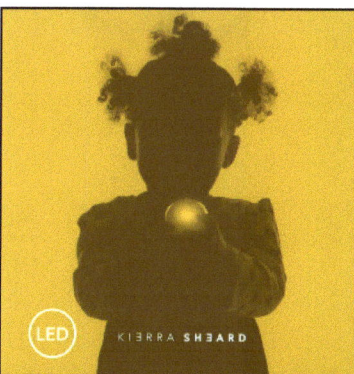

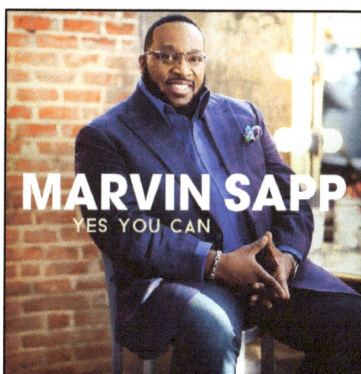

LED
KIERRA SHEARD

MARVIN SAPP
YES YOU CAN

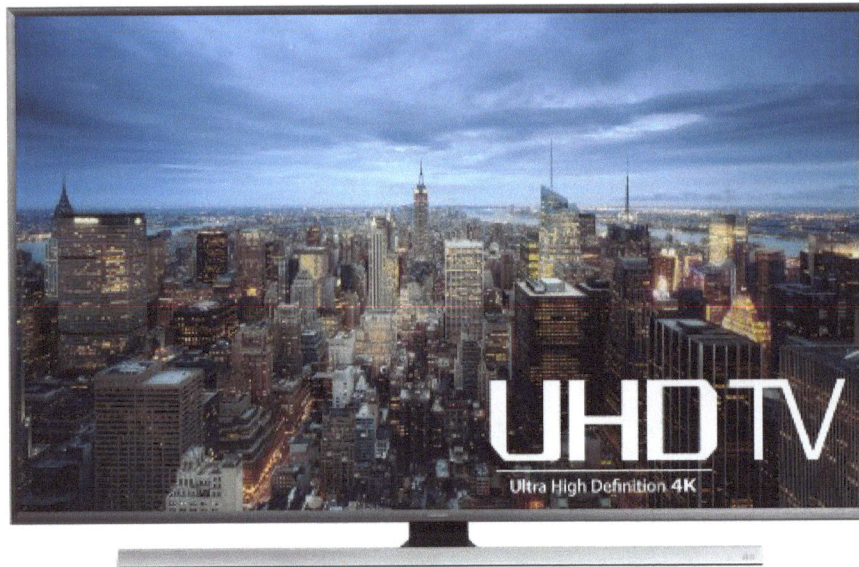

①

NEW ELECTRONICS

A LIST OF SOME OF THE PICK'S THIS MONTH.

BY JEFF WALKER

②

③

① Samsung - 55" Smart 4K Ultra HD TV

Check out the Samsung 4K Ultra HD TV, the world's newest addition to PurColor Technology. The Samsung 4K Ultra HD TV also allows you to watch TV using the built-in Wi-Fi. You can stream music and download apps on the TV.

② Apple TV

Get access to instant entertainment with the Apple TV. Just connect to the Internet and stream movies, listen to music, and access a wide variety of other content. You can also connect your iPhone or iPad to the Apple TV for streaming more apps.

③ WowWee - MiP Robot

The WowWee MiP 0825 robot is a robot that plays games, drives, dances, battles, balances, responds to motions. This is all controlled remotely controlled by a compatible iOS or Android cell phone for ease of use. The dual wheels allow smooth, simple mobility.

④ LG - ChromeBase 21.5" All-In-One - Intel Celeron

This LG ChromeBase 22CV241-W all-in-one computer features built-in wireless networking and a 1.3MP webcam, which makes it simple to chat with family and friends over the Internet. The Intel® Celeron® processor is reliable for everyday computing.

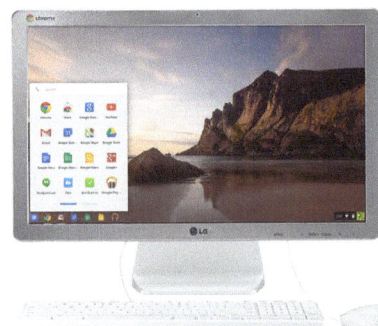

④

The biggest thing to happen to iPhone since iPhone.

iPhone 6s

www.apple.com

Local Entrepreneur's Working

HIGHLIGHTING LOCAL TALENT'S DOING WHAT THEY DO BEST
BY CREATING A BRAND FOR THEMSELVES IN THE MIDWEST.

by Cheraee C.

Sonya D'Zines is a stylish boutique located in East-pointe, Michigan. For over 32 years, Sonya has been designing prom dresses and praise dresses. Sonya has sewn clothes for gospel entertainers and Detroit celebs such as Twinkie Clark, Kierra Sheard, Anna Marie, Kenya Moore, and Barbara Rose Collins. She also has a clothing line called Virtuous Women Wear.

If you are interested in designs by Sonya, you can reach her at (313) 316-2216 or Facebook her at Sonya D'Zines.

Sonya D'Zines

KaSiris Xavier

KaSiris Xavier is an entrepreneurial cross platform smart applications developer. By the grace of God he builds everything from Android apps to smart TV networks. KaSiris is also a freelance photographer who takes pictures throughout the metro Detroit area.

If you are interested in any of KaSiris's services, you can Facebook him @Ka Siris Martez Xavier.

A Powerful Message from God

ANNA MARIE MCCUTCHEN GIVES GOD THE GLORY AFTER HER LIFE WAS TURNED AROUND FROM A MESS TO A MESSAGE.

by Anthony Ambrogio

From a Mess To a Message is both a memoir and a self-help book. Gospel Singer Anna Marie McCutchen provides examples from her life and appropriately selected scriptural quotations to illustrate that sometimes the mess IS the message.

She shows how even our darkest days have a purpose unto God and that, if you let go and let God lead you, your life can have purpose and meaning. Readers can use her text to make a message out of what they mistakenly believe is the mess of their lives.

You can find more books & music from Anna Marie McCutchen on her website: www.annamariegospel.com

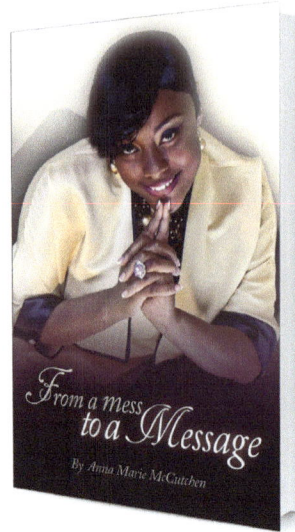

From a Mess to a Message
By Anna Marie McCutchen.

Available from Amazon.com and other online stores

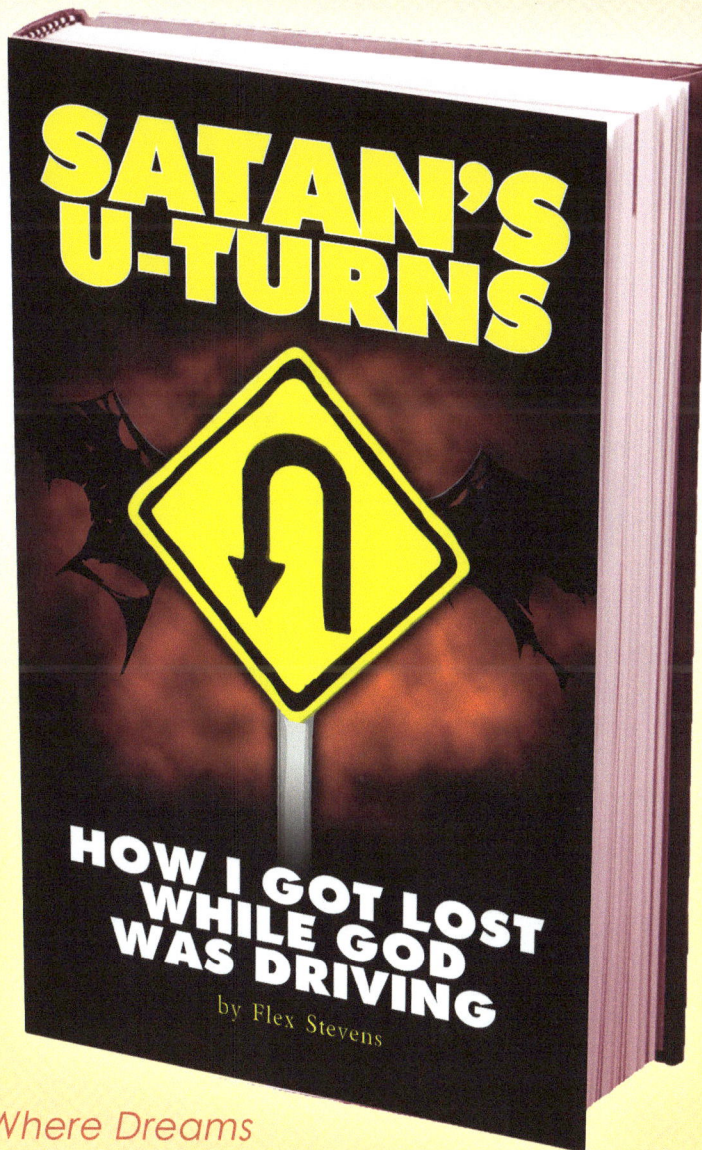

Pastor Marvin Sapp's Journey

WHILE ON THE JOURNEY FOR CHRIST PASTOR MARVIN SAPP GIVES A BLESSING TO THE WORLD WITH HIS SONG "YES YOU CAN".

by Anna Marie

Marvin Sapp, a world renown Gospel Singer and preacher, is one who has persevered through many hard trials. The loss of his wife has been one of the hardest to cope with namely. He continues to travel the country with his ministry.

An anointed man of God who pours out passionately with preaching the Gospel and also more expressive through singing. Pastor Sapp is from Detroit. He currently Pastors a church in Grand Rapids called Lighthouse Full Life Center. His latest single is entitled "Yes You Can". This song is sweeping the nation and has a massive impact on almost everyone who has a strong faith in God and refuses to give up.

MARVIN SAPP
YES YOU CAN
DjBj & Big Sean

Helping the Community

MAKING A POSITIVE TRANSITION TO PURSUE A BETTER LIFE BY WALKING WITH CHRIST AND HELPING OTHERS.

by Cheraee C.

Keith Goodwin is the founder of One K Studios located in Detroit, Michigan. One K is an entertainment agency inspired to help poets, singers, models, dancers, writers, and musicians.

The meaning of One K is "all are one." For more inquiries you can contact Keith on Facebook @ONE K STUDIOS, email @onekstudios71@gmail.com, or by phone at (313)656-9399.

Keith Goodwin

Incarcerated Youth Ministries ©

It is most important for those who have enjoyed some measure of success to give back to their communities. One such person who is making a large contribution is Anna McCutchen. Anna works with us ministering to incarcerated youth who are housed in Wayne County.

Anna brings her skills as a counselor twice a month and often performs at worship services for detained young men and women between the ages of 11 and 20. Giving back and paying it forward are very important to Anna, and she does so with great grace and style.

MISSION

Being a Mouthpeace For Jesus means that you openly profess the word of God. The purpose of MPFORJ is to spread the gospel of Jesus Christ around the world through what we call, Apparel Evangelism. It's your choice whether or not you use your mouth to speak peace or guile. If you vow to change your words and begin to profess the things of God, you will change your life and current situation. We can all be a Mouthpeace For Jesus; all we have to do is speak the word of God.

MOUTH PEACE FOR JESUS

T-Shirts
Graphic
Designs
www.mpforj.com

Detroit's Own Kierra Sheard

HAS A NEW EP ENTITLED LED AND IT'S TRULY ONE OF THE BEST GOSPEL ALBUM'S IN THE COUNTRY AND ONLINE.

Photography by Anna Marie

Kierra Sheard is a young international Gospel singer who's home church is Greater Emmanuel located in Detroit, Michigan. She continues to encourage all age groups from around the world with Christian music and entertainment. Kierra Sheard is a leading young lady for female vocalists in the Gospel music genre. Kierra Sheard has a prosperous clothing line called, "Eleven 60".

Kierra Sheard's newest EP entitled LED. It's sweeping the nation. Her latest album release is "Graceland". She has a remarkable contemporary flavor with heartfelt meaning in her lyrics. Hats off to Kierra Sheard, who is born into one of the most talented families.

Dear God, heal those with cancer. Amen.

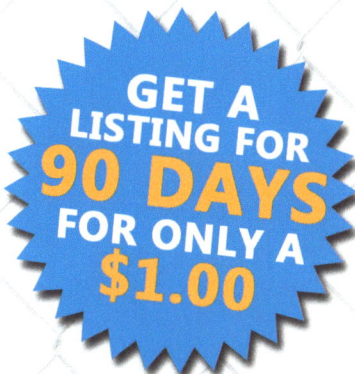

Spotify News

INDIE ARTIST PERRIN LAMB EARNS OVER $56,000 FROM ONE SONG ON SPOTIFY WITHOUT A RECORD DEAL.

by Semaja Turner

Perrin Lamb is an indie singer-songwriter from Nashville. He's been in music for over a decade. Never signed to a record or publishing deal. He decided to distribute his music thru CD Baby, which an indie music distributor that distributes for independent artists.

In January of 2014, a song that Perrin wrote called "Everyone's Got Something" was selected to feature on the Your Favorite Coffeehouse playlist on Spotify by their editorial team. At this time, Perrin's song had been out for about a year and wasn't doing that well in the industry. It wasn't until the song hit the playlist and boom. The song went from hundreds to millions of plays in no time.

As of today, the song has gained about 13 million streams worldwide. Perrin's was paid for getting over 10,929,203 streams from Spotify for his song "Everyone's Got Something". From that, he earned a total of $40,131.55 (which was left after CD Baby's 9% distribution fee.) Perrin also earned Mechanicals and digital performance royalties that make up the remainder of the total $56,000.

Walking by Faith in Prosperity

HOW WALKING BY FAITH LEADS TO THE PATH OF PROSPERITY FOR ANNA MARIE WITH HER NEW BLESSING FROM CHRIST .

by Cheraee C.

Walking by faith leads to the path of prosperity. When you don't give up and move in faith, God moves on your behalf. God has given to everyone one of us a measure of faith. We should focus on being abundant in spirit.

3 John 2 reads, "Beloved I wish above all things that thou mayest prosper and be in health even as thy soul prospereth.

For six years, I've been laid off from the Board of Education. I testify that God has been providing for me thus far and has been giving me the strength to get up and get my blessing every day. I have been traveling, making gospel music, and writing books for over eight years. My gifts are my livelihood. My music can be found on iTunes, Google Play, and other major online outlets. My books are on Amazon and Barnes & Noble. My mother Carolyn Elizabeth McCutchen has taught me to persevere in life and always keep God in my vision.

I've been (From a Mess to a Message) and now I am determined to (Aim High.) God has allowed me to give my heart to book-writing and song-writing. Beginning

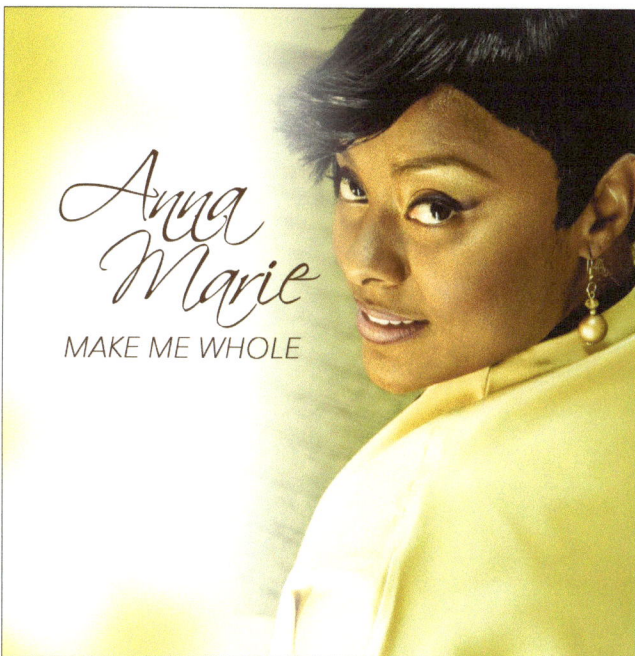

June 2015, he even gave me an interest for worshipping him through praise dancing. God takes pleasure in using people who have been rejected, people who suffered, looked over, talked about, hated, misunderstood, etc. He gets the glory out of turning their mess into a Message. All praises belong to Jesus for the things he has done. Faith works!!!! To God be the glory!!!

TOP 10 CHARTS

TOP 10 DIGITAL SINGLES AND ALBUMS
JANUARY 1, 2016

MARVIN SAPP - BLESSING THE WORLD WITH HIS HIT SINGLE.

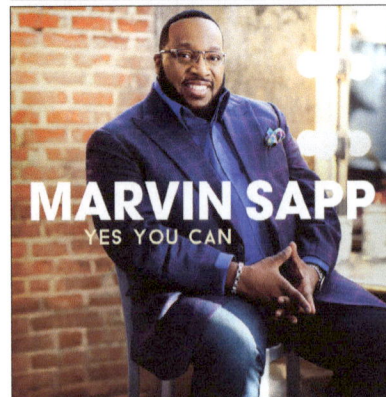
TOP 10 SINGLES
CHART OF THE MONTH

No.	Artist - Song Title
1	MARVIN SAPP - YES YOU CAN
2	CANTON JONES - FILL ME UP AGAIN
3	MARY MARY - GO GET IT
4	LE'ANDRIA JOHNSON - SOONER OR LATER
5	TAMELA MANN - I CAN ONLY IMAGINE
6	CE CE WINANS - WE WELCOME YOU (HOLY FATHER)
7	SHIRLEY CAESAR - WHEN YOU PRAY GOD ANSWERS
8	ALEXIS SPIGHT - ALL THE GLORY
9	ANNA MARIE - MY TESTIMONY
10	DEITRICK HADDON - SINNERS (SAVED BY GRACE)

TOP 10 ALBUMS
CHART OF THE MONTH

No.	Artist - Album Title
1	CE CE WINANS - THY KINGDOM COME
2	KIERRA SHEARD - LED (EP)
3	CANTON JONES - GO MODE
4	KIRK FRANKLIN - WANNA BE HAPPY?
5	TAMELA MANN - BEST DAYS
6	LE'ANDRIA JOHNSON - THE AWAKENING OF LE'ANDRIA JOHNSON
7	MARY MARY - GO GET IT
8	SHIRLEY CAESAR - GOOD GOD
9	ANNA MARIE - LOVE LIKE JESUS
10	DEITRICK HADDON - MASTERPIECE

ALBUM REVIEW

Good God

ARTIST: Shirley Caesar
REVIEWER: Cheraee C.

Shirley Caesar, a well-respected legend, who is both a singer and preacher. She has many awards and achievements. Her "Good God" record is just one of her most outstanding albums that have blessed us all. I have had the privilege of enjoying her in concert. This iconic artist travels the world spreading the gospel and making a positive impact on all age groups.

Shirley is also known as the queen of Gospel music. As she continues to touch the lives of many, may the Lord keep her well with divine protection. Thank you, Pastor Shirley Caesar, for sharing your preaching and singing with us all.

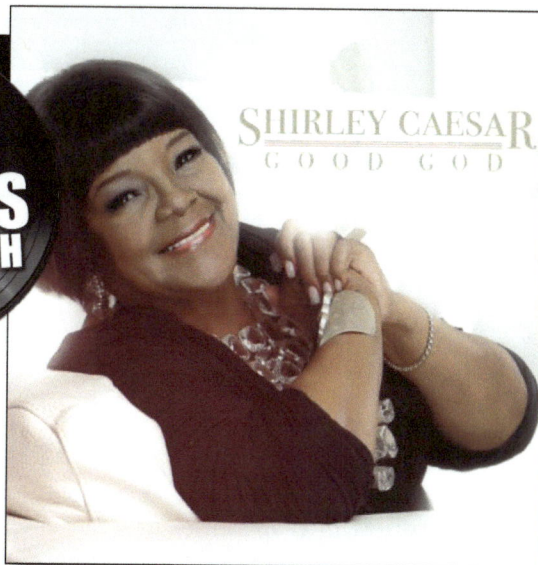

TOP 3 ALBUMS THIS MONTH

SHIRLEY CAESAR
GOOD GOD

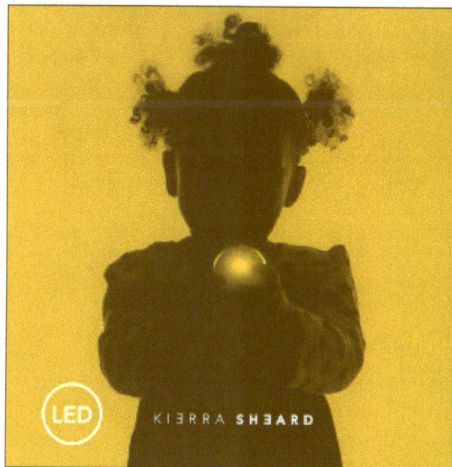

LED-EP

ARTIST: Kierra Sheard
REVIEWER: Jason White

Kierra Sheard is one of the wittiest musical artists for her age bracket to bring such contemporary style music combined with her anointing. Thank God for her style of music that she brings to our young generation. Thanks for blessing us with your music.

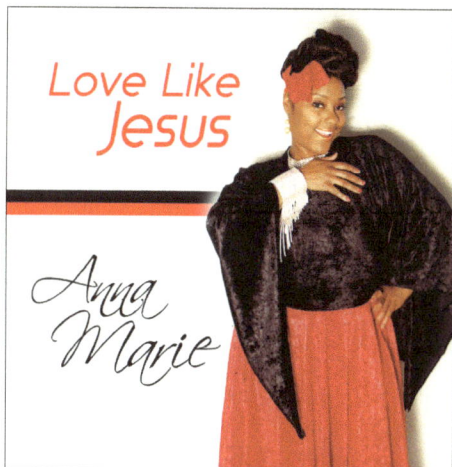

KIERRA SHEARD
LED

Love Like Jesus

ARTIST: Anna Marie
REVIEWER: Suzy Stafford

I can tell that Love Like Jesus came straight from the hurt. Anna really felt the Love of God shed abroad in her heart. The world needs love. If it were not for the Love of Christ none of us would be here. People see Christ when we demonstrate our love. It must have been crucial for Anna to have written those songs and sing out of the Love that the good Lord has placed in her.

Love Like Jesus
Anna Marie

Overcoming All Odds

JIMAVIS AND JIMAZHA TRIUMP AND CELEBRATES NEW LIFE AS SUCCESSFUL WOMEN BY WORKING HARD AND PRAYING HARD .

by Jimavis Hatchett

I grew up in a single parent, drug abused home. Many would say that alone made me a statistic. Living in a free world (doing what I wanted to do), I started to venture off into selling drugs, drinking, smoking weed, and skipping school. I was no stranger to prayer as I learned at an early age to pray for my mom to be safe and drug-free. That was my job most days.

My grandfather had strong faith and always taught me to honor thy mother and thy father. (Ephesians 6:2) The other thing he taught me, that I would never forget in his words "GET YOUR EDUCATION". As I was always a good student with good grades displaying honors most of the time, I lost my way. For some time, I strayed off doing things that I surely was not proud of. I knew my grandfather was praying for me. I was not aware that I was in a mess, that I needed prayer for myself.

At the age of 17, I was introduced to the Teen Mom lifestyle. I had no idea how my life was about to change. Single I was, trying to care for this baby that needed me. My prayer GOT DEEP!!! I began to speak to GOD on a regular basis. He saved me from my free life, saved me from jail time, saved me from death, and allowed me to come through in one peace. As he turned my life around, I GOT UP!!! It wasn't easy at all. I spent many of my days crying from the pain of the struggles. I found myself quoting scriptures like… This too shall pass (rephrased from Deuteronomy 28:1)…..The Lord is my Shepard, I shall not want. (Psalm 23:1) Times started to get easier, not because the obstacles were not there, but because God gave me the strength to get through it. (Psalm 29:11) I WORKED HARD AND PRAYED HARD!!!

With my baby catching the bus early in the morning, I was able to complete high school as well as get a job as a nursing assistant. This was a milestone for me. Not only was it to get me back focused on my dreams to becoming a nurse, but it was a good paying job at the time that allowed me to provide for my family. Through it all, I kept pushing and praying. Since high school, I dreaded going to college because I thought I couldn't make it.

In 2002, the year my dear grandfather died. I stood up on faith and started at WCCCD. Trying to keep a balance of school, work, and parenting, I started off slow in the beginning. As 2006 was coming to an end, I decided to let some things go and let GOD. I went to nursing school full time. He never let me go hungry or in need. He put others in place that they could be a blessing to me. (Deuteronomy 28:8) We were up at 5am every morning to get our day started. From school, helping the daughter with homework, going to after-school programs, and sports; many days I just passed out on the couch. I made sure that regardless of whatever I had going on I would continue to be the best mother I could be and be present.

Through it all I am forever grateful. I have completed nursing school and currently practicing as a registered nurse since 2009. My daughter graduated from high school and joined the United States Navy (proud Navy mom). My mother has been clean and serene for 14 years and counting. PRAISE GOD!!!

Gospel Hip-Hop Rapper

CALIK STILL SIK IS TELLING HIS STORY ON HOW CHRIST SAVED HIS LIFE WHEN EVERYTHING WAS LOOKING BAD FOR HIM .

by Calik Still Sik

Let's see where to start? How about the first time I wrote a rap for a poem recital in my 8th grade english class. Didn't know how that would turn out and was a little nervous. But after I did, the class went crazy, I was too excited! So from then I continued to and been rocking since 1984. That was 26 years ago; over two decades of knowledge and wisdom in this hip hop world. I've seen many mc's come and go. I also understood why so many have rose and fail. Obtaining this information helped me to develop an eclectic style that I can call my own where my life and music marry together.

Over the years I have been on stage with some of the best artists in the game. I have also had collaborations with them as well. Along the way I ran into mishaps that altered my career and my life. I say that because I always believed in truth and realism, so my music reflected my life and my life reflected my music. Meaning whatever I talked about I did it, and it came along with all the bad that happened. But my passion for music was always hard driven; I did music no matter what I was going through. At some point I fell victim to the streets and became lost in my environment up until 12 years ago.

Certain circumstances repeated itself in my life where I went from being on top of my game to losing almost everything and was stripped down to nothing. But I still thank God for my wife and kids. God drew me in with his love and my passion for doing music. Then turned it around so that my passion is for him, and he uses me and the gift he gave me as a tool and vessel to reach others. The beauty of my music is it remains laced with the truth and realism, and now my music and my life marries together with Christ. I have a whole new approach than I did before: my deliverance from drugs, alcohol, and a street mentality which now gives me a second wind and a whole new life. I thought that at this age I would be hanging up the mic and working behind the scenes, but God says no! He's given me longevity and I feel I can go on twice as long understanding the language and the center of the social lives of the youth that makes me approachable and marketable in this industry.

My music gives a little of what they want and more of what they need. I have released four projects of my own such as: "Still Sik, Special Deliverance the mixtape, The Soul Rehab, and now Secular to Gospel." I have also produced other upcoming artists and possible ministers in their projects with mentoring, fellowship, and guidance. I help them to line their lives up with their music to push Christ, promote life, and produce faith. Examples include Edify a kid out of Plymouth, Michigan, FLOW another inspiring minister from Midland, Michigan, Yung Saint from Detroit, Michigan, and a very determined young man from Wixom, Michigan by the name of Whop and there are more to come if God's will. So my heart just wants to see the doors of this "life encouraging genre" be kicked wide open for instance when you poke a hole in a dam and it starts to leak the pressure from the water behind the wall will eventually break the dam's walls if I may and the Gospel will flood the world! MY name is C.A.L.I.K. synonym for Cant Always Live In Kaos! Support the movement lets bring "Secular to Gospel."

NEXT 2 GLOW

SUDANA FOWLER THE MOUTH PEACE FOR JESUS.

After writing music all of my life, I finally received the name Mouth Peace from God in 2012. It was after I decided to take music ministry serious. I asked God, and he told me this is who I am. When it comes to ministry, music, spoken word, etc. I am an Oracle for God. I was lead by the Holy Spirit to branch off and do ministry through clothing design.

The term God gave me is Apparel evangelism. It's an opportunity to witness through clothing. Therefore combining graphic designs and T-Shirt printing, it became MPFORJ custom apparel and design. I create and provide design services for others.

There are numerous other things that I do in God's kingdom including preaching the Gospel, prison ministry, poetry, and writing children's books. To contact me go to www.mpforj. com My fan page is Mouthpeace Instagram is mouthpeace4Jesus

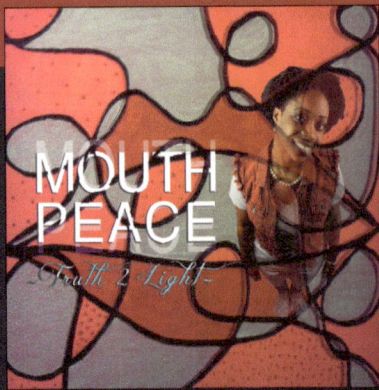

Mouth Peace - Truth 2 Light
(Mouth Peace for Jesus)

From the Streets to Salvation

HOW LAWRENCE E. JOHNSON FOUND HIMSELF IN TROUBLE WHILE DEALING WITH THE DEVIL. BUT HE SURRENDER AND GOT SAVED.

by Lawrence E. Johnson

Lawrence Edward Johnson II was born April 7, 1973, on Detroit's Westside. He grew up with his three sisters and a young nephew in a single parent home, where his mother worked two full-time jobs to make ends meet. Growing up impoverished, in a household that lacked little to no adult supervision, Lawrence soon found himself caught up in the street life that lures so many young men to the drug scene. "I saw guys my age with all the cash and the fresh gear, and I said to myself, "I want a piece of that." I was recruited by some of the older cats in the 'hood who got me started selling crack. It was all good till I started to get jammed up every time I turned around."

"Back in the 80's, the system was more lenient on younger offenders. I had a rap sheet a mile long with every kind of offense: drug possession, weapon possession, endangerment, recklessness, etc. I beat everyone, but then I got caught with 350 grams of cocaine. I was charged with drug possession with intent to distribute and deliver which carried a max of 25 years. Frankly, I don't know how I beat those charges..... but at that time, I had applied to my current position at Cobo Hall. When I got called into the interview, the manager asked me about the charges on my clearance. I told him to what I believe to this day is what Jesus had to me to tell him. I said, "Sir, I know I have charges on my clearance, but please take into consideration that those charges say "pending" next to them, not "guilty." In January 2016, I'll have 20 yrs. at Cobo Hall.

"After being acquitted on all charges, I started to move away from that lifestyle. I still wasn't living right, but God's grace was upon me. I had side-stepped any prison time or felonies on my record. What was amazing is that in all of it, I was attending church faithfully with my mother. She was the one committed to the church; I was just committed to getting her there and back. I was still drinking, smoking weed, getting high and running the streets. I hadn't yet had a personal relationship with Jesus Christ though I was faithfully in the church every Sunday with Mama. I just thank God for my mother's prayers that covered me."

SNAP SHOTS

Email Your Snap Shots to
annamariepraise@gmail.com

A Divine Floral Shop

DESIGNING AMAZING FLORAL ARRANGEMENTS FOR ALL OCCASIONS ON THE EAST SIDE OF DETROIT.

by Cheraee C.

Kozy Floral is a trendy flower shop located on the east side of Detroit, Michigan at 14945 Harper Avenue. Kozy specializes in floral designs for all occasions especially weddings and birthdays.

If you are interested in floral arrangements for any occasion, you can contact Robert Jones at (313) 333-9275 or Facebook him @Robert Jones.

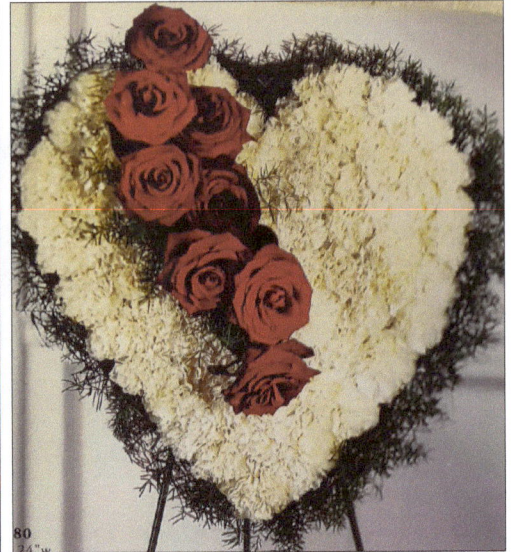

WE HAVE THE LOWEST PRINTING PRICES IN THE NATION

250 EVENT TICKETS
FULL-COLOR ON BOTH SIDES ON THICK UV COATED 14 PT

only $45

1000 BUSINESS CARDS
FULL-COLOR ON BOTH SIDES ON THICK UV COATED 14 PT

only $25

1000 4X6 CLUB FLYERS
FULL-COLOR ON BOTH SIDES ON THICK UV COATED 14 PT

only $65

Need a Design? Add $20 for Business Card or $40 for Flyer

2x5ft VINYL BANNER
FULL-COLOR IN or OUTDOOR BANNER w/GROMMETS

only $99

5000 BUSINESS CARDS
FULL-COLOR ON BOTH SIDES ON THICK UV COATED 14 PT

only $99

2500 4X6 CLUB FLYERS
FULL-COLOR ON BOTH SIDES ON THICK UV COATED 14 PT

only $85

CHECK OUT MORE SPECIALS & ORDER ONLINE ANYTIME: WWW.5DSPRODUCTIONS.COM

1.888.718.2999   5DS PRODUCTIONS® THE PRINT MEDIA CENTER.

THE ALL NEW STYLE OF MAGAZINE-BOOKS

ANNA MARIE
MAGAZINE

www.ingramcontent.com/pod-product-compliance
Lightning Source LLC
Chambersburg PA
CBHW040021050426
42452CB00002B/71